Like Water in the Palm of My Hand

Like Water in the Palm of My Hand

Poems by

Lois Roma-Deeley

© 2022 Lois Roma-Deeley. All rights reserved.
This material may not be reproduced in any form, published,
reprinted, recorded, performed, broadcast,
rewritten or redistributed without
the explicit permission of Lois Roma-Deeley.
All such actions are strictly prohibited by law.

Cover design by Shay Culligan
Cover image by Javier Miranda
Author photo by Erin Perre

ISBN: 978-1-63980-110-7

Kelsay Books
502 South 1040 East, A-119
American Fork, Utah 84003
Kelsaybooks.com

For Sydney James

Other Books by Lois Roma-Deeley

The Short List of Certainties

High Notes

northSight

Rules of Hunger

Acknowledgments

The following poems—or slightly altered versions of these poems—were first published in the following:

Antiphon: "Anxiety and Television News" (with audio recording)
Artemis: "Reading James Baldwin for the First Time"
Best Poem: Good Men Project (reprint): "Otherwise"
Blue Heron Review: "Like a Road Rising High Above the Sea"
Blue River: "Teach Me How I Should Forget to Think"
Bosque: "This Is Not the Life I Thought We Would Have"
CapsuleStories: "The Cell Phone Rings Inside My Pocket," "Like Water in the Palm of My Hand"
Comstock Review: "The Hands Have a Language All Their Own (for Eileen Shiff)"
Constellations: A Journal of Poetry and Fiction: "At the San Xavier Mission"
Geology of Spirit: A Photo-Poetic Collaboration: "Be There No End to the End of this Night" (originally published as "Be There No End to the End of this Day"), "Now That," "Empty Spaces," "How to Be Rooted," "If When," "The Love Poem (I Can Not Write)," "If I Were Smarter, I'd Be More Afraid" (reprinted)
Glass: A Journal of Poetry (Poets Resist): "Kiss, Kiss" (first published under the title "Kiss, Kiss, Senator Mitch")
Glint: "Spell Bound"
Gyroscope Review: "Absence in Five Parts"
Here: A Poetry Journal: "How to Forgive," "Like This Story," "Grateful"
Insight II: "What It Is or How to Get There"
Italian Americana: "In My Brother's Recovery Room"
Mom Egg Review: "Riding Past the Cemetery in April"
Muddy River Poetry Review: "The Virgin River Speaks of Loneliness," "Distance and Regret"

The New Engagement Literature and Art Journal: "The Only White Woman in the Room," "Dyslexic Me," "Moon Star Looks Into the Night Sky and Sees You There"
New Millennium Writings (anthology), "Be Here Pow" Issue: "Why Moon Jellyfish Won't Speak of Cancer"
New York Quarterly: Without a Doubt (anthology): "Like Water in the Palm of My Hand" (reprint)
Odes and Elegies: Eco-Poetry from the Texas Gulf Coast (anthology): "The Love Poem (I Can Not Write)" (reprint), Lamar University Literary Press
Open: Journal of Arts and Letters: "Emily Dickinson Travels Between Two Points in Time"
Orbis International Literary Journal: "Night Driving with Narcissus and Echo"
Panoply: "This Is What a Young Man Looks Like When His Heart Is Full Grown"
Parentheses Journal: "Telekinesis for Beginners"
Post Road: "I Came Here for Some Answers"
Prime Number Magazine: "The Fainting Man in the Painting"
Quiddity International Literary Journal and Public-Radio Program: "Caliche"
Red Savina Review: "Among the Red Rocks of Sedona, a Soldier's Wife Leaves No Stone Unturned"
Rust + Moth: "Sleepwalking Through the City"
Silver Birch Press: "New Ink" (originally published as "If I Added to the List")
Slipstream: "Who Can Bear This Much Truth?"
South Florida Poetry Journal: "Quick Enough"
SWWIM: "Ghost Mother"
TAB: The Journal of Poetry & Poetics: "Like a Stranger at Your Door" (with audio recording)
Twelve Mile Review: "Like a Map to the Middle of Nowhere"
WORDPEACE: "[In This Cynical Time]"

Yes, Poetry: "After Hearing How the Judge Didn't Want to Ruin the Rapist's Life"
Zoetic Press: "The Reporter"
Zone 3: "If I Were Smarter, I'd Be More Afraid"

The poem "Grateful" was a top ten 2019 *Tiferet* Writing Contest finalist. For the *New Millennium Writings* XLV contest, the poem "Why Moon Jellyfish Won't Speak of Cancer" was also a finalist.

The poems "Be There No End to the End of this Night" (originally published as "Be There No End to the End of this Day"), "Now That," "Empty Spaces," "How to Be Rooted," "If When," "The Love Poem (I Can Not Write)," and "If I Were Smarter, I'd Be More Afraid" (reprinted) were part of the exhibition *Geology of Spirit: A Photo-Poetic Collaboration,* with fine art photographers Patrick O'Brien and Cyd Peroni, and with poet Rosemarie Dombrowski (https://www.geologyofspirit.com/). The poems "I Came Here for Some Answers" and "The Virgin River Speaks of Loneliness" were written in response to the work of visual artist Beth Shadur. The poems "What It Is or How to Get There" and "Why Moon Jellyfish Won't Speak of Cancer" were written in response to the work of visual artist Cherie Buck-Hutchison. The *Vice-Versa* anthology "Illness as a Form of Existence" republished "Why Moon Jellyfish Won't Speak of Cancer," "Absence in Five Parts" and "In My Brother's Recovery Room."

Grateful acknowledgment is made to the Arizona Commission on the Arts for their support during the time when many of these poems were written.

My deepest gratitude, as always, to Sydney James and Marianne Roccaforte-Gardner. And to Peter Deeley Sr, Peter Deeley Jr, and Melissa Deeley Rothlisberger—for now, then, always.

Contents

One: Shifting Shadows

Particulars	19
Telekinesis for Beginners	20
Sleepwalking Through the City	21
If I Were Smarter, I'd Be More Afraid	22
Like a Stranger at Your Door	23
Teach Me How I Should Forget to Think	24
Ghost Mother	25
Anxiety and Television News	26
How to Forgive	27
If When	28
Why Moon Jellyfish Won't Speak of Cancer	29

Two: Failing Into the Problem

At the San Xavier Mission	33
Like a Map to the Middle of Nowhere	35
Empty Spaces	36
Be There No End to the End of This Night	37
After Hearing How the Judge Didn't Want to Ruin the Rapist's Life	38
I Came Here for Some Answers	40
Absence in Five Parts	41
Night Driving with Narcissus and Echo	43
The Fainting Man in the Painting	44
What It Is or How to Get There	45
The Cell Phone Rings Inside My Pocket	46

Three: Ghost Whispers

Like a Road Rising High Above the Sea	49
Spell Bound	50
The Love Poem (I Can Not Write)	51
Riding Past the Cemetery	52
Outtakes from the Movie of My Life	53
The Virgin River Speaks of Loneliness	57
Dyslexic Me	58
The Only White Woman in the Room	59

Four: Nodes and Edges

Reading James Baldwin for the First Time	63
Like Water in the Palm of My Hand	65
The Reporter	67
New Ink	68
Moon Star Looks Into the Night Sky and Sees You There	69
Distance and Regret	71
[In This Cynical Time]	72
Quick Enough	73
Emily Dickinson Travels Between Two Points in Time	74
Among the Red Rocks of Sedona, a Soldier's Wife Leaves No Stone Unturned	75
This Is Not the Life I Thought We Would Have	76
The Hands Have a Language of Their Own	77
In My Brother's Recovery Room	79
Kiss, Kiss	81
Poem in Which I Rescue You	82

Five: Compass Points

Otherwise	85
Who Can Bear This Much Truth?	86
Caliche	87
Like This Story	89
How to Be Rooted	90
Grateful	91
This Is What a Young Man Looks Like When His Heart Is Full Grown	92
Now That	93

One

Shifting Shadows

"Time flies over us, but leaves its shadow behind."

"We travel, some of us forever, to seek other states, other lives, other souls."

Particulars

one kangaroo. one sad story. one street, one way, up or down. doesn't matter where you go, you always wind up. with an uncommon note, silver and blue. like the harmony of speech and silence. or the solitary heart refusing to open. but what about that kangaroo? you really want to know, don't you? how things get pocketed into other things. the one and only, the specific,
the different.

Telekinesis for Beginners

First, massage lavender oil
onto each temple, then notice

the wine glass on the kitchen table,
empty now of all meaning.

Feel energy flowing through muscle and bone;
focus all intention.

Now close both eyes.

The candle will slowly burn down into itself.
Cypress will charge the air.

Now blink twice.

A school bus levitates off the ground.
Spoons melt inside a porcelain cup.

Mountains will quake at the magnitude
of such power.

But there's so much more
I have to move.

Consciousness is a fragile thing.

Sleepwalking Through the City

Often I find myself waking in strange places—
in a neighbor's bathtub, at the paupers' cemetery,
on the last car of the light rail.
The doc said it comes from watching too much news—
the fragile mind can't cope. Tonight
here I am again, alone and confused,
standing barefoot, in the heart of Phoenix,
at the Zen garden, *Ro Ho En*.
It's late. There's black tar on the bottoms of my feet—
I must have been walking for hours
with eyes wide open, seeing nothing
but this unraveling dream
tucked somewhere in between
Central and Third Ave.
The night took me to the golden Buddha
squatting on a slab of rose quartz stone.
He winks and grins at me:
nothing is lost in the universe.
Suddenly everything I thought I ever knew
is rushing at me—

It's not the first time I've been taken for a fool.
My throat is dry. Sweat runs down my back.
I decide to ignore him,
focus on how I've always loved
the hidden places
of this city—named for a bird
which consumes itself in flames, then, rising
from its own ashes, is reborn
just to do it all again.

If I Were Smarter, I'd Be More Afraid

Perhaps it's too early in the morning
or maybe it's still very late at night?
Suddenly words fly out of my mouth
like startled birds scattering before a hard rain.
Call them back
says the winter storm. And I know I should
rescue those fleeting thoughts,
care for these lost and hungry pilgrims
shivering in the wind.
If I were smarter, I'd be more afraid because

outside ghosts dance
in a circle of crackling white light.
They feel their way
into living bodies, settling at last
deep inside their bones.

Suddenly the sky splits open. Trees explode.
But then I remember
on the rooftop of this house, a lightning rod holds fast;
the copper wire reaches up,
even as it runs down
straight through the heart
and into the storm soaked ground.

Like a Stranger at Your Door

I'm across town now.
My nightgown's torn. The bottom hem
catches on the bindweed which pushes up
and through the crushed gravel beneath this window
of a small room on the first floor of Mercy Hospital.
My hands frame my eyes as I press them against the cold glass.
Is this what they mean by *lucid dreaming?*

You're lying in bed
like a caterpillar caught in its own silk.
Nurses come and go
talking of yesterday's television show.
You recognize no one

not even your own daughter
who leans over and whispers *hello.*
Faces without names turn over in your mind
like rocks carried by a fast moving river,
the force of nature
wearing edges smooth and round.
The years unwind. It must be someone's fault.
The nurse tells your daughter it's time to leave.
You turn your face to the wall.

Tomorrow, your first born will drive to work, step into the parking
    lot.
Her high heel will disappear into the newly laid asphalt
and it will be then that she'll remember the lesson of dark matter—
how a dying star leaves behind a black hole,
an invisible wound in the heart of deep space,
the place from which light can never escape.

Teach Me How I Should Forget to Think

holy light
falling through the window,
hushes along the floor, reaches for the dreaming bed
where I lie like a restless child
inside damp and tepid sheets. Red-faced sun,
bursting now from the cloudless sky, do you know

how very hard it is to be a human being?
To pick and choose one's way among the many
crowded streets which lead
to broken bodies hanging in the square?
to sirens stopping at my door?

even as the day scrapes and bows,
dropping to one knee like an actor
stage whispering to the retreating dark,
let me rest in your waiting arms and kiss the cheek
of every misplaced hour—

were we not made for more and yet just for this?

Ghost Mother

Egyptian Woman Disguised Herself as a Man for 43 years
—*The New York Times*

If you had asked me, I would have told you
why I dressed in these pants and tunic,

tied a green scarf around my close-cropped hair,
smoked cigarettes, spoke rough and low—

why I harvested crops,
hauled cement, lifted bricks,

cleaned the dust and dirt off a thousand shoes
with nothing more to think about but how the day would end.

My daughter survived and I
was never beaten again.

Now, walking through the maze of back alleys,
I set my back against the wind. I'm a ghost mother—

memories float me through time
to our small house, the one with two good chairs,

an old radio humming on the kitchen shelf,
and my little girl playing on the bare floor. I am

a pearl shadow,
standing at the stove, smiling

at pigeons simmering in the pot who seem to smile back.
I fill their stomachs with rice and herbs,

and now they bob up and down
on a roiling sea of cinnamon and cloves.

Anxiety and Television News

My lungs hurt. I'm not breathing.
So, here I sit, alone on a narrow bed,
making hand puppets appear and disappear
between the lamplight and the wall.
Stretching both hands wide open,
I cross both palms, one over the other,
waving each finger in, then out,
again and again
the shadow bird
dips and dives in dizzying circles,
flies across the room. Suddenly and without permission
a panther lurks inside your calloused skin.
All we know of hope surges in the air.
My knuckles lock in battle;
the panther swallows the sparrow whole.
And now I know, don't I?
how a shadow sounds, half-singing, half-wail.

How to Forgive

If there were a chart or grid
arranged in horizontal rows
according to the ways and means
of how we should forgive,
would I close my eyes and point
to any square
like it's a game of pin-the-tail
on and of deep wounds,
mine or yours?
Would I then open my eyes and say
here is mercy, there is forbearance,
and on *this* spot,
tucked all the way at the corner of the page,
the one framed by blame and spite—
is *absolution.*
But isn't forgiveness a way of letting go?
the release of hurt into the still night air
like a body giving up the ghost
rises from its bones and, atom by atom,
fuses star dust and soul.

If When

you are sleeping
the rain poured off the roof,
into tin gutters and, finally, down to a lake
ringed with stars. This is the dream
you dream night after night
of being transparent
rolling water—
you travel, now, then, always, in a straight line—
piercing time.

Why Moon Jellyfish Won't Speak of Cancer

I suppose I should start more slowly,
work up to it, draw you in,
tell you a smart story
about a wolf limping down a country lane
and how the animal is chained to a gray bearded beggar
who is toothless but properly kind
and how they're suddenly overtaken by a wind
so powerful
it blows them both clear across the ocean
where they are trapped forever on an island you never dreamed of
but fear might actually exist.
But that won't do,

it won't tell you how the words
"cancer" and "I have" take on a life all their own.
This tale won't take you to that elsewhere place
where time creates a silky pocket
and shoe-horns you inside its pouch
or how you'll press fingertips to the wall
of that translucent membrane
which divides the *just-you* from the *just-world.*
Perhaps if I mouth the words

"we are not alone"
to the trembling moon jellies glowing in the dark,
floating to the surface of an eternal sea garden,
their luminescent hearts would sing out to me
there is language beyond language—
would the sting shock you?
would you believe me then?
if I said I am always afraid now
of beginning this kind of story.

Two

Failing Into the Problem

"We are afflicted in every way, but we are not crushed...."

At the San Xavier Mission

You worry too much, I say.
It's my job, you say.

As we begin to make our way
up the dirt trail toward Grotto Hill,
we see, in the distance, stone lions waiting at the gate,
jaws open in perpetual roar.

I'm not dead yet, I say. Good, you say,
now hold onto my arm, steady yourself.

We're half-way up the mountain
having just left the old mission church
known as "the place where water appears."
And I want to tell you that I still believe

in divination,
the way a dowser grasps the Y-shaped branch
with the palm of each hand,
and walks slowly over the ground until
the rod dips, then dives deep into the earth
and there, leaping from the dusty, barren sand
water overflows and the desert is made green once again.

But then we make our turn, and there,
in the middle of this desert, is the grotto
where, on a makeshift table of slab rock,
two dozen candles flicker, and

tucked under each candle,
cards, letters, tattered photographs—
prayers for those we two will never know.

I scribble on a slip of paper,
fold the note in half, then halve it again, the corners
forming a small envelope in which I leave
just one name. You hold your breath,
tight inside your chest, afraid of what will happen
when you have to let it go.

Like a Map to the Middle of Nowhere

The Mermaid sign above the coffee shop
near Third and Central Ave flickers
like the broken porch light
of my childhood home. My friend,
I'm not sure I'm ready to tell you what happened.

Now I slip into the parking lot, kill the engine,
watch the heat rising from the blacktop
like sea serpents on a map to the middle of nowhere.
"Here be dragons," I whisper
to the crosswalk sign which beeps *go, go, go—*

the sound reminds me, not of monsters,
but the relentless tweaking of a circus clown's nose.
I squeeze my eyes shut to drown out the sound. Suddenly

I'm seeing little girls everywhere…
Three hold hands under the shadow
of a sweet Acacia, chanting
songs about smelly socks and pink overalls.
One chews the inside of her cheek,
two others throw a yellow ball against a brick wall.

And now, pushed to answer the one question
you have to ask, all I hear is the catch
in my voice; the click of my words
tumbling against each other,
falling hard on the tile floor.

Empty Spaces

Between the lake and river
hemmed by pine trees and small boats
there is a highway leading
to an abandoned house.
And in this house there is a mirror
hanging on an adobe wall. And the wall
guards a window
which frames this view
of a deserted barn with a slanted roof
sitting on the parched ground of a vacant lot
during a cloudless day—
Now supposing I memorize this picture,

would I get the colors right? name them
burnished slate and *porcelain clay,*
gypsum dust or *sapphire blue?*

Could I measure the silence?
valuate its depth and width
like the account left
in fossil leaves, or mineral bone?
You are supposing I should know

the poetry of empty spaces,
the distance between the ripples
and the halos around a winter moon.

But supposing now
all I see is dark spaces
around and in between
that house, that wall, that which invades our dreams—
what could be. And what it means.

Be There No End to the End of This Night

Just as the arrow weed, stripped
of all intention, asks the single leaf
to curl inside itself just as
the desert sun draws a shadow line
across the unsuspecting ground
dividing sadness from sorrow
just as the wild horses bend their heads
to drink from the cool river of doubt
while the Mesquite trees shimmer gold,
their leaves trembling in welcome
just as the wind moves through
and around and within this night
just as spirals of honey bees hum,
the thrum and lightning strikes me.

After Hearing How the Judge Didn't Want to Ruin the Rapist's Life

for T.S.R.

Here you are, stopped short,
waiting in line for the light to turn green
at the entrance to the 101 Freeway.

You kill the radio—wonder what's wrong with the guy
in your rear view mirror, the one who screeched to a halt,
stopping a fraction of an inch from your bumper.
Now you see through the white smoke spewing from the exhaust
a girl standing on the street corner.
She holds a wilted cardboard sign, the letters bleeding
into each other from the winter rain which falls from the sky
like the hammer of an angry god. So

rolling down the window, you wave 2 bucks at the kid.
You do this because you can't stand seeing
how her long brown hair is pulled, tight and hard,
back from her face by a blue rubber band;
how her wet hair falls, almost deliberately, into a fine point
all the way down her back, like an exclamation mark
at the end of a *National Enquirer* story
everyone reads in the supermarket while waiting to check out.

You tell yourself the girl's going to be okay—
someone will come and rescue her. Or maybe
she'll walk down these side streets,
and find that one house among so many houses
where there will be, no doubt,

a small lamp with a fluted silk shade sitting on a small table
in front of a picture window,
the light shining through the glass onto the stone path
which will welcome her home.
But that wind! You hate the wind—

how it lifts her hair like the hand of someone who,
not long ago, grabbed the back of your neck, hushing
Be Still.

It's getting darker now and it's raining hard and
the light just changed; now
the SUV in back of you is leaning on the horn and
yeah, you're late for work again
and you're almost out of gas and

you are very sure now
the cops will be coming by real soon.

I Came Here for Some Answers

At the top of the Grand Staircase
in Bryce Canyon
the hoodoos call to one another—these rock waves,
crests of limestone, siltstone, dolomite, mudstone
paralyzed by time, patiently resist the dark night sky.
I came here for some answers.
But if these stone towers and red spires
know anything, they're not telling me.
I've never understood the beauty
of destruction. Shiva's third eye of wisdom.
Those Tibetan monks who destroy sand mandalas
to get healed. The millennia of wind, water and ice
having their way with me. This moment
which will never come again. The weathering
of my life into smaller and smaller pieces
until there is nothing but this silence
whistling past my ears.

Absence in Five Parts

i.

After a week of radiation, I'm a goddess.
I'm cleaning closets and cabinets, decluttering my life,
kicking the habit of holding onto useless things.
I am creating a universe of perfect order.
So into the trash I toss
"Owl Drink to That" and "Sip Me Baby One More Time,"
wine glasses bought by a younger self.

ii.

Make room for the new, my mother always said,
and then
throw out what doesn't belong.
Now I'm cramming mismatched socks and crusty flowers
into the mouths of plastic sacks
like baby birds demanding to be fed.

iii.

She'd be proud I haven't flinched
while organizing my life into piles of yes and no.
So picture books from the Uffizi, a poster of the first Star Wars
    movie,
an "I Heart You" stuffed bear I once held, gently,
against my mutilated breast—each and all
get pitched into the box marked *Savers Thrift*.
I take a cleansing breath.
I've done good work tonight.

iv.

But I'm wondering what can't be reused with a little more care?
Like the cashmere sweater with tiny moth holes,
the one I mended with invisible thread,
the one she thought I'd never own.
Then suddenly, and without warning,

v.

there's a tenderness underneath my ribs;
pulling up my shirt, I look at blotches on my skin and—
though I know I'm lucky to be alive—right now it seems
my soul is pushing through my chest, and
it will leave behind nothing
but these broken blood rosettes.

Night Driving with Narcissus and Echo

You're talking to the rearview mirror,
like a cartoon character on methamphetamines,
speeding on this wet road
through the stippled light of the damn trees,
the rain on the concrete a slick reflection of green.
My mouth makes fog circles on the window pane,
and when I speak the words bounce
back to me, slapping my face—

stop; stop

and you keep chattering on about how,
in the end,
everybody will *love* your style;
they'll adore your endless array
of sky blue oxford shirts
and pin rolled trousers,
they'll envy the spit and shine
of your wing tip black shoes and,
when they reflect on this forest,
growing darker with each turn,
they'll know, you are so very sure,
these forest sounds are but an excess
of wind slamming through the trees
or water rushing over dead leaves.

The Fainting Man in the Painting

After viewing The Crucifixion of St. Julia by Hieronymus Bosch

Perhaps he just couldn't take seeing a woman
becoming a saint
crucified on a cross,
her bloody hands and retching eyes
reaching up toward a heaven
he no longer believed existed. Or maybe
it was the sudden clap of thunder
bursting inside his head,
that made him dizzy. Or the ringing
inside his ears sounding like a thousand wings,
bats spiraling out of the mouth
of a deep and forgotten cave.
He grew cold and numb,
saw the aching auras
of zigzagging silver lights, a whirling
galaxy of shimmering stars—
and so he fainted,
dropping into the waiting arms of two men
he thought were his best and only friends.

What It Is or How to Get There

I'm thinking of you
as I'm loitering in front of the *Mystic Bazaar*
eavesdropping on the tourist
who is asking of each and every passerby
which way is *the* best way
to the "energy vortex" and "healing orbs"—
I've stopped for a moment, somewhere in between
the town near Oak Creek Canyon,
a few miles down from screaming children
riding the rock water slide, quick and cold
over a stretch of slippery creek bottom and
the place where you now live. This thin voice
of a grocery store clerk stealing a day from work
sounds a lot like you. Tapping the map
the woman demands from these perfect strangers some direction
she can count on.
It's true I have nowhere I want to go
but I won't answer and besides
I don't really know—now this woman
in the spandex pants and the black bolero hat
with fringed red balls which shimmy when she talks,
stops in front of me, leans against the window.
There are sobs between sips of diet soda
which she drinks from a plastic jug and now
she looks more like me after one of our long talks
—not lost, just a tourist in my own life.
Closing my eyes, I concentrate
on the electronic pipe flutes bursting from the loud speakers and
block out her incessant breathing.
Now I wonder if and when
I should go into the store, take a picture of my aura,
buy those aqua quartz wind chimes, have my palm read
and now it's not you I'm thinking of—
not now, or ever again.

The Cell Phone Rings Inside My Pocket

I won't answer.
I never do.
Instead, I place the heartleaf philodendron
on the kitchen windowsill
as if the rising winter sun has come
to celebrate this moment of possibility.
Tomorrow I'll clean the backyard
stripping the willow bark of dead leaves
piling them onto a cord of split wood
and a grate of concrete.
Snow will fall onto my wild hair.
How should I think of love now?
My fingers, numb from cold,
fumble for a match.
Then I blink, twice. The snow will fall
suddenly and without warning,
pushed by a fierce wind,
it drops against the back door
like a fighter slumped in a corner
after going down for the last count.
Picnic benches, fence posts,
even the ceramic gnome you set in the garden,
will be covered
with the singleness of cold, the push of winter.
I'll turn toward the house, then back again,
my boots making a full circle in the snow.
A gray squirrel will jump onto the pyre,
eyes staring up into my bloodshot eyes,
head tilted at an odd angle,
curious about what I might do next

Three

Ghost Whispers

"Wherever you go, you meet part of your story."

Three

Ghost Whispers

Recover the forgotten parts of your story

Like a Road Rising High Above the Sea

Marianne has seen me study
the seduction of early winter—the rivulets of ice crystals
cracking along the windowpanes and how
the snow shadows fall onto the gables of my neighbor's roof.
This coldness, you say, beguiles me.
Yet I have told my friend that a quiet life
is like a road which rises high above the sea.
But she won't let me go. And so
somewhere between two continents, not lost,
but simply far beyond belief, she travels to me.
Together we sit in a pale blue room
on a paisley sofa, drawing near the roaring fire. And we drink
glass after glass of plum wine and eat with our fingers
from bowls of sliced apples and purple figs.

Spell Bound

Me: Before they married, what did she do for a living?
You: She was a pretty girl.

She was
the applause of a hard rain
falling into the street, and soon after,
the slap of new shoes on wet concrete;
She was
the shimmer or the shine
of a dozen sequined mouths
stitched onto the back of a leather jacket;
the slice of orange and the leaves of mint
swirling around the edges of a water glass;
the flick of a cat's tongue, pink and pointed.
She was
the welcoming flash of blinking neon signs;
the long boat leaving the harbor
sailing past the horizon line
of a man's body;
She wanted the hunger
inside the bird's belly;
the pause before evening prayers;
the ground of no sorrow
reeling under a ribbon sky.

The Love Poem (I Can Not Write)

Inasmuch as trees huddle together
in groves of whispers, their roots
reaching down
into the innermost part of the earth, and inasmuch
as moths are blinded
when they can not use the moon
to navigate the night, inasmuch as
light travels in waves faster through water
but never enters
the deepest known point in the ocean
even though the largest library in the world burst open
with its 5.5 million maps, inasmuch
as each had a legend, but no key
to unlock the mysteries of us
inasmuch as this story goes.

Riding Past the Cemetery

The kids tell me it's bad luck
to breathe in the air of the dead.
But I'm more fearful
of Spring's unpredictable heart—
how the purple mallow and common milkweed
scramble along the ground,
their roots pushing through and down
rocky soil,
growing and growing,
as if they know where I am going.

Outtakes from the Movie of My Life

for Kerry

1.

We're stuck on a raft lurching down Snake River,
having come a long way just to find some peace.
In this aerial shot of steep canyon walls
and white water tumbling over jagged rocks,
we're floating—
dark specks of solitude and longing.

2.

Suddenly, the movie jump cuts
to the close-up of us
drinking from the same canteen.

3.

But we both know the camera doesn't love us.
Our faces swell and redden
under the summer sun, filling each frame
with too much sorrow.
Now the lens refocuses itself

4.

and I crack a few jokes.
You're my best friend and so,
throwing your head back, you laugh.

5.

The birds flying high above our heads
squawk out their warning.
Now the image changes again

6.

and there I am running down cellar steps.
In the dark we hear a frantic breathing.
There's a homeless man
crawling through your basement window.
We're afraid—we're always afraid—

7.

he's come to steal the scene,
hungry for applause.
The camera pans left
to stacks of musty magazines
then right to piles of mildewed books,
finally resting on the thief sitting right between them.
A flashlight hangs from his mouth.

8.

He writes on a yellow pad,
the words glow iridescent in the damp air
as if it were a script—

9.

of the party where we first met.
In this tracking shot
my hair is long again. My hips are swaying
inside that silk dress. *Some Kind of Blue*
plays through the backyard speakers.
Someone is swimming in the deep end of the pool.
While I'm standing on the over seeded lawn,
a drink in one hand, joint in the other,
you're on one knee, scratching the throat of a stray cat.
Strange voices surround us.
In the middle of the crowd
loneliness is a just another face among the rest—

10.

mine, the only one you'll recognize.

11.

My high heels sink into the soft grass,
staining the tips a soft shade of green.
Now you come behind me, surprise

12.

whisper into my ear: *What year is this?*
I can't remember.

13.

Time fades in/fades out.

The Virgin River Speaks of Loneliness

so deep
are narrow canyon walls,
cut into the heart of Zion
while the cottonwood trees and box elder
stand bewildered and confused.
Where does the wind come from?
and why do these waters rush along?

Look up.
Time leaves a message
on these sandstone cliffs
no traveler can read.

Dyslexic Me

Sometimes the beginning and end of a word
whiz(   )zes on by me so quickly
it's as if
I'm standing on the side of this long road
when it's been raining all day and all night and
I'm pulling my rain jacket cl( )ose to my chest,
shoving my hands in both pockets just to keep warm,
wondering, now, which way I should be going,
when, suddenly,
three short bursts of a pneumatic whistle
from this 12 geared, turbo charged, 40 ton, 80 foot MACK truck,
screams
step back—
and I jump into the weeds, stepping on broken glass and now
all I know is
something big is about to pass me by,
heading for the mouth of the dark tunnel
which is buried underground and beneath the riverbed ,
and the *thing* won't stop
for anyone or anything and now
all I can do is guess at what it all might mean
when the steel disc wheels crush through the puddles,
the diesel exhaust slaps the side of my face,
when there's only the head(   )lights,
then only the tail(   )lights, and
every(   )thing in(   )between
is nothing
but swirls of dust and fog.

The Only White Woman in the Room

I like these black and brown women
and they like me. So when they said
Come With. I said, Okay. Sure. Why not. Make no mistake,
this isn't even a poem
about seeing something, being something.
It's not even a metaphor about what I didn't know
or where I journeyed to or where I came from.
It's just a story about not knowing

on this particular evening in the early part of winter
when we all gathered in the big ball room
of the university which sits on the edge of the desert
gossiping about the big boss and how this work place
just won't give us a break and how
we really should be moving on soon;

when these beautiful women, dressed like angels of God,
in flowery silk dresses that float across the room, a hymn of grace
rising out the mouths of a church choir; when these women
whose spiky heels on bare tile announce,
a woman of consequence is coming for you.
So that's the scene. Got it?

My friends are talking and laughing with me
before the speeches start and while I'm sipping my drink, and then
now this is the part where you must pay attention—
at this precise moment and for no reason at all
I suddenly notice I'm white—
Oh-My-God-I'm-White!
what if they notice how white I am?
then, in a panic, I try to tuck in my whiteness
like it's something stuck on the back of my shirt and
I try to fold it all in, all that whiteness,

'cause I don't want to be embarrassed by something
I should control. Still and much later
when I recount the story, making fun of myself as I tell it,
my Latina friend just smiles at me and
I finally stop talking.

Four

Nodes and Edges

"Destiny itself is like a wonderful wide tapestry in which every thread is guided by an unspeakably tender hand, placed beside another thread and held and carried by a hundred others."

"Our life is composed greatly from dreams, from the unconscious, and they must be brought into connection with action. They must be woven together."

Reading James Baldwin for the First Time

Sitting on the concrete stoop of my aunt's row house,
underneath a broken window, a book propped against my knees,
my life was more mystery than fact.

And with every turn of the page, I searched for clues,
as if there was some undiscovered map
of how to be, what to do.

Not everything that is faced can be changed,
Mr. Baldwin said,
but nothing can be changed until it is faced.

Junkies pissed against the wall. But I won't notice.
Mothers leaned out apartment windows,

screaming at children playing stick-ball in the street.
But I don't hear. Then I saw you turn the corner,
you're a man who looked like he knew where he was going.

Hey Sweet Pea, what's shakin'?

and my heart gets to racing as you flashed by.
I memorize everything you do—

how you scooped the rubber ball from the concrete with one hand,
tossing it back to Fat Tony and Little Mike

with the long arc of your left arm,
or how your upper lip curled—rock star style—as you nod

to Mario and Big Jim slouching near the roach coach; and you
    always bowed,
just a little bit from the waist, like an orphaned prince,

when greeting the old men sipping espressos
outside the *Four Aces*. And when you finally left the neighborhood
I remember how you said good-bye,

the side of your hand sliced the air in two,
like a shark's fin cutting through the waves.

Much later when I grew to be a woman
and tattooed the secret of my sex
in blue ink over the scar on my breast, it read

like a long scroll of warning—

Like Water in the Palm of My Hand

It hurts to look
at the medieval cathedral sitting high on a hill
and then walk through the rough doors
only to discover the delicate fresco inside its dome
darkened so by centuries of candle smoke and prayers.

Gray-faced angels poke their wings through dingy clouds,
pointing at the heads of shipwrecked sailors
bobbing in a grimy sea of loss.
But why am I surprised at the vivid reflections

on the mosaic stone floor, swirling around both feet;
how the rosettes of muted greens, cobalt blues, wine reds
could be an obvious answer
to the only question my heart is afraid to ask?

Courage is needed to look up again
into the vaulted ceiling, which pushes and pushes skyward,
while wondering how those stone arches could carry the weight
of so much of my own longing.

Suddenly, the tapestry hanging on the back wall billows
like a friendly wave from another life,
the one I could have lived. Now I begin to see
into the design this scene
where a terrified doe jumps into the forest of Ash
while three hounds nip at an archer's heel.

And now, like water in the palm of my hand,
I'm dropping through time,
understanding more than I can know. . . .

But the eternal now quickly slips away
leaving me alone in this shallow winter light.
And I can't explain how I came here
or why this ancient weaving deeply wounds me.

Perhaps it was the wind—
or something like the wind—
coming through an open window,
which released an arrow from the archer's bow
piercing my heart like this and just so.

The Reporter

In 1965 on that day when the scent of snow
still lingered in the Ponderosa pines,
your mother cried all morning—
Viet Nam was a long, long way from here.

From your parents' small brick house, you walked
through narrow streets, past a 7-11 store, you walked
down into the town of Prescott, Arizona,
until the blisters on your feet bled—

until suddenly, you explain, it was like a scene from an old movie
when you found yourself standing all alone
in front of a white building.
You have come to do what you must do.

When you got to the recruiting station you tell me
how you cup both hands on the window pane,
take a good look inside and
just as my feet are shifting, pointed toward the door,
you grab my arm, look deeper into my eyes,
continue on with your story
about how the window glass felt so warm
in that late afternoon sun and
how surprised you were to see your own face
reflected in the window,
so imperfectly round it was, like a boiled egg,
and now your black eyebrows make one long line,
a continuous sentence, just like this one,
the report you won't ever get to make.

New Ink

If I got another tattoo
it wouldn't be designed by Bang Bang or Dr. Woo—
no single continuous line
of delicate blue will snake around my wrist—
no poem or lyric song
will slither up my arm, coil around
the nape of my neck.
My new ink won't be in Mandarin,
no slender strokes will rise above my left breast—
Winter's eye is closing. Since you left me
I've learned
a few names for the color red:
candy apple, cherry, bittersweet.
Now I squint through the smoke of my cigarette,
check my phone for texts I will never read,
my finger deleting each with a majestic flourish.

Moon Star Looks Into the Night Sky and Sees You There

Breaking the boredom
of unemployed hours,
I drain the last Bud from the last six pack when
you show up, asking *Do you want to party?*
I've been waiting all night

for trouble to find me.
You who call yourself *Moon Star,*
giggle as you climb into my truck
and onto my lap.

Now a sleek Mustang pulls alongside,
honking at the two of us.
It's way past midnight
but all the cars are still cruising Central Ave.

Someone smashes a beer bottle in the street.
Someone throws the first punch at a bar.
Like a song ending on the right note
the Mustang fades down the street,

its triple plated Mag Wheels
glinting under the halo of a street lamp,
the eyes of a saint rolling in ecstasy.
Then I kiss you

and it's more like a dare than a promise.
The scent of lavender soap
in your cotton blouse mingles
with the smell of a wet dog.

Red blotches
the size of whole continents
erupt on your neck and shoulders.
Suddenly you clear a spot
on the foggy windshield.

Now taking off your bra,
unzipping your too tight jeans,
you whisper into my ear, *take a good look
at those stars in the heavens*. And now
the night sky is really spinning.
See? you say,

it's the Hunter with his sword
then pushing your hand deep inside my pants,

oh Lord!
how you laugh.

Distance and Regret

I don't know how I found myself
lying in my neighbor's empty bath tub

curled into a ball
like a kitten trying to keep warm.

Someone keeps shouting at me
wake up…

But on the back of my eyelids, there is this scene—
one bird flitting among three trees.

Then it's me who's flying
over rooftops and city streets

in a helicopter with no doors and broken seats.
We're soaring over mountains and valleys now.

Helicopter blades make shadows
on the patchwork ground,

a pinwheel illusion
of green fields/white sand/small figures…

Children in cages. Parents weeping at the gate.

I snap a few pictures, jot down a few notes.
The camera's eye adjusts itself

to a finer understanding of distance and regret.

[In This Cynical Time]

You're almost at the end of your speech now
explaining to me how the world really works.
I've been trying hard to focus. But then
a young couple stops in front of us. When they kiss
even the giddy leaves shake with happiness.
Now you begin to speak once more
stabbing your forefinger at the air.

Yes, but no
I'm with the lovers now
having followed them down to the bridge.
Your eyebrows twist like a bowline knot,
the one sailors use when the ocean swells
and small boats tug at the docks. Hiding myself in shadow
I'm watching the sweethearts kiss again. And again
my breath quickens
when the lovers hang a lock on the grillwork,
and it's my own heart that is humming
like the wings of a small bird suspended in mid-air
as they throw the key, high and wide,
into the deepest part of the river Seine.

Quick Enough

Tonight I'm driving Famous Guy
from my college to Sky Harbor airport.
This late no one's on the road but the two of us
and the echo of the day
when in every class at every hour he talked
and talked about empty book shelves and lazy readers,
about how time moves, why people don't change.

Now I roll the window down, wishing it would finally rain.
Then suddenly, as if it's a pop quiz, I'm stopped short
by a red light and he asks
Do you know the difference between quick and fast?
His head's bobbing from side to side
like that plastic bulldog, tiny spiked collar and all,
stuck on the dashboard of my neighbor's car.

When the light snaps green, I step, hard, on the gas.
His glassy blue eyes look away.
But I'm a magician now
tapping the top of the steering wheel
like it's a silk hat and—*presto, change-o*—
pulling out of the dark
with a flash and puff of white smoke, it's
now I see you, now I don't.

Emily Dickinson Travels Between Two Points in Time

I am the also of your life,
the farthest town on the
discolored map, the point to which
you always turn, in love
with distance. I know the signs
of place—here I stand on that which was once
a nothing bit of road, too thin
even to hold the dust
against my shoes—but this mirage,
you want me to be
is like desert thunder
which too soon expands like water
in a lake of air! So just
as it may seem to you unwise
for me to ever talk of *us,*
I'll count the days of when and since
your desire became too much.

Among the Red Rocks of Sedona, a Soldier's Wife Leaves No Stone Unturned

As we hike the short, steep climb into the saddle points
of red rock country, I am uneasy. Since you came home
I search for the magic words

which will open your heart, make you whole.
You won't speak much. You don't sleep
in our bed. You wander for hours. I don't know where you go.

Now the sky above us is a relentless blue.
I lean, hard, between two walking sticks, hunched over
like some bewitched character in a fairy tale—

a servant girl? a beggar? Cursed
by a sorcerer who's always jealous and never tires
of turning handsome men into trees

and all the beautiful women into doves.
Iraq is a long, long way from here.
But, across the wash, near the granite cairns,

there's a low growl rising from the bottom of your throat,
escaping between your teeth, and
now it's me who's terrified. But the sound

of the wind in Pinyon Pine and Juniper leaves
fairy dust sprinkled in your hair. From the lips
of penstemon and wild lilies still in bloom,

an incantation is sung just for you, my love—
and I ask its mighty power
to grant us the one wish I have left.

This Is Not the Life I Thought We Would Have

Desert winds blow through my car.
The windshield's cracked. I'm cracked—
Inside my head, Madame Butterfly is singing
one beautiful day. The air conditioner wheezes
its disbelief. I'm almost late
for the new job I already hate,

but I haven't worked since forever.
Now the temperature gauge is rising.
I turn the heater on, hoping the radiator
won't boil over.
This is not the life I thought we would have.

That's what you said to me this morning,
sitting on the steps with your head cradled in your hands.
I am trying to imagine our future

when I'm not counting
gas and milk and paper towels,
pennies saved in the jelly jar,
hives erupting all over my skin.

Now my bald tires squeal like pigs stuck on barbed wire.
Plastic melts into my thighs.
The morning sun rises, blood red and perfectly whole.
Then the razor thin outline of Superstition Mountain
slices across the sky, leaving me with a numbing pain
which sinks into me, and how you won't let me believe
this is an omen, my one and only
promise of relief.

The Hands Have a Language of Their Own

for Eileen Shiff

i.

Mourning doves flying from roof to fence, from fence to tree
ride along the tongues of air.
There are mute angels who write in ink on the palms of your
 hands.
Open them.

See the creases: life-lines, love lines—the ungiven speech
punctuating folds of linen cloth,
Shabbat silver. Two slender fingers

snapping white candle into flame. How your mother would
have looked,
her eyes widening,
at the one blue glove in your lap.

Once you dreamt of daughters. Running
a thumb around the edge of rising yeast,
you cradled bread, then tasted salt.

Come winter, you would make a bouquet
of small faces—pulling them
close to your own, breathing them in.

You would hold onto love.

ii.

Say *Shalom*.
Say the sound. Release it.
Find a place,
lay the book open. Turn the pages.
By now, you should know…

iii.

Mother. Sister. Teacher. Wife.
Let it go.
The hands do not forget; they always remember.
Now pick it up. Now put it down.
Make it even. Make it smooth.

iv.

The sky is a blank slate. Write what you will.
Today children are walking through the petting zoo reciting their
      lessons. The monkey house
is dark and dangerous. It's late November. Your fingers ache.
      You feed the baby wolf.
My hands cover your head. The clouds hold still.
      Only the leaves move, cling to our shoes.

In My Brother's Recovery Room

Years ago you watched every Superman show,
instructing me on the particulars:
how the Man of Steel can press coal into diamonds;
that only green Kryptonite will bring him to his knees.

But when you told me your hero can split himself in half,
occupy two places at once, I became the little sister of unbelief.
You fooled me so many times, my brother, with

Santa Claus eats little girls and
the Devil lives in the dark space underneath the bed—
I never knew which of them was true.

It's late now in your small hospital room.
You're floating between this world and the next.
The doctors broke you open,
cracking your rib cage, pulling away the flesh,
exposing heart and lungs.

Tonight it's you, Nick, with the "S" on your chest,
a careening line of stitches, cat gut and dried blood;
black circles under each eye,
like the dark face of the moon, forbidden places
no one wants to go. And suddenly I'm remembering

the day a nail went through my foot
and you carried me three blocks home.
Even superheroes get afraid, you whispered
as I sobbed into your neck. Now

between sips of water, you see angels—
streaks of sapphire blue, vermillion, gold,

and one who gives a message
without words in the landscape of pure white.
Now I know all of it is true.
Time breaks itself in two. Love leaves in us a deep, sweet scar.
You tell me *write this poem.*
I will, Nick, I will
just this once and ever after, every time always for you.

Kiss, Kiss

When Doris Day dances around that movie bedroom
in "The Man Who Knew Too Much,"
swirling around in her pretty white dress, smiling and singing
Que Sera, Sera—
as if nothing really matters because
What Will Be Will Be—I always want to scream. Look
when love or cancer, or the crazy guy with a gun
runs towards us, smacking his lips
kiss, kiss—
we're always surprised—
but *goddammit,* never close your eyes.

Poem in Which I Rescue You

I'm lifting you out of the here and now
and opening the door to the other side
of how good life is supposed to be.
Now I'm shoving you through—
dead bolting lock, jamming lever, throwing away key.
Even after all your pounding, sill to sash,
your fists begging, bloody knocks,
I won't let you back in.
Then, while you're pushing and grunting,
I'll jump kick the peephole,
drive my heels into the floor,
and, after I wedge a chair underneath the knob,
I'll slip a note underneath the thinnest crack—

This is your new home.

Five

Compass Points

"Show not what has been done, but what can be. How beautiful the world would be if there were a procedure for moving through labyrinths."

Otherwise

From this distance, my husband seems so small.
Like water over mill wheels, he moves
through dreams in one direction. If I call

to him from this great height: *we
had a life no one thought practical,*
Will he look up and will he answer me?

Love and work will kill him. I've seen his eyes
study the clouds, heavy with ridicule,
too late. But what if there were better lives,

Some way we always think that it should be? Our days
filled with a furious constancy,
rise through the rain. We are not what we became.

I have looked into the palm of his hand
cupped under the well-pump and don't know why
he doesn't scream out loud. The farmer

and his wife—Tom and Jane—two marks
over one grave. Now he sees my face
in the light on a pool of standing water...

From a whisper of dark,
Honeysuckle in the meadowland,
I breathe out the last of my heart—

We have lived as if this is commonplace.

Who Can Bear This Much Truth?

I do not wish to be
a mourning dove with pearl gray eyes
pecking at snails in the sorrowing ground.
Or even the beak of the bird grabbing seeds from the earth.
You won't see me fly

below our small apartment window
when sirens grip me by the throat
and the jackhammer drills its way
into concrete, pavement, rock.
I'll pound my head against the wall,

as if this, and only this,
will make the noises stop.
Across town, on the other side of the Salt River,

someone sets a car on fire.
Doors explode. Tires burn.
And as the carcass smolders, smoke rises
in black plumes like fingers
of a demon child
scratching names onto a crystal clear blue sky.

Caliche

In the Sonoran, the fickle desert rain
never comes when you need it—
but when the wind picks up, it pours itself out
empties itself of the black sky
rages down dry gullies and aching river beds
like a promise. Or a curse,
leaving behind *caliche*—white rock soil—
the ground which refuses to be tamed.

Tonight, after working for hours in our garden,
I pour myself a glass of red wine,
and look among our too-full shelves for something light to read
—a good story always takes the edges off the day.
From the other room, TV laughter fills the house.
Just then an almost forgotten book leaps from the top shelf,
drops near my foot.

Wedged between its pages, a fading Polaroid. Stuck.
On the back is a note penciled, long ago, by our teenage son:
Be Home in an Hour—

the top of each cursive *"H,"* noble curly-q's and loops,
reaching up, hopeful and unafraid.
You call to me from the other room but this photo takes me back—

It's New York again with its endless winter.
We're young and cold and out of work. Again.
Dark rings circle my eyes. Your fake leather jacket
droops on your shoulders.

The baby's cheeks are fever red.
You're rocking him on your hip.
At the unemployment office, the three of us inch our way on line
toward the window cage where the beaky nosed clerk
interrogates you,
while her pigeon eyes peck away at my skin.
So I drop both hands to my sides,
let her have her good look.
When I start to cry—whimper really—you whisper:
Don't.

Like This Story

Become as sunlight
traveling from deep space

into the prism hanging on the back wall;
separate the colors of want and need.

And when you manage to

break free of this earth
—and all those bastards dwelling on it—

to leave behind the hungry eye refusing to be filled
and greedy hands taking what they should not own,

fly past the clouds. Then turn around,
look back at this blue planet

and count every imperfect being
as your own. Wait there until

love is the only thing that moves
with and between and into

this body once called you.

How to Be Rooted

Even if I stood in the snow without any shoes
while I shook myself from sleep;
and even after you, my love, suddenly appeared
and together we inhaled the bitter midnight air,
lungs aching with every syncopated breath—
how long would it take for both of us to know
the reach of cold is not absolute?

Grateful

For the drama of bread rising.
For the pomegranate waiting to be opened,
and recklessly spill itself out
into a glass bowl; and for its accomplice,
the radio sitting on a shelf high above the kitchen window
crackling sweetly because it knows something I don't.
For the clearness of a blue night sky
requiring nothing from us
but to look up. For the great while
as I remember the word *meadow*
with its invitation of longing. For the day
I found you
standing in a field of dandelions,
the winged seeds floating the long distance
between then and now.

This Is What a Young Man Looks Like When His Heart Is Full Grown

There you are in the photo, not quite 18.
It's winter and we've crossed the causeway
hours ago. We park at the beach
in field lot 5 which sits outside the boundaries
of the Fire Island seashore. We're not talking,
huddled together inside your father's grey Buick,
but we're listening to the idle of the engine,
cries of sea gulls circling overhead.
Suddenly, you square your shoulders,
lean back against the seat, rest your wrist on the steering wheel.
There's a certain peace in this bitter cold.
Now the wiper blades scrape back and forth
making half-circles on the windshield
as though the full arc of our lives
is set before us in one neat repeating pattern.
You don't notice as I snap this picture of you
looking out the car window,
watching the snow falling, hard and furious,
into the ocean. You stare
at a future coming at us like a gigantic wave
crashing over the sand. *Take this,* it roars,
and see if you can live.
I remember being 16 and so in love with you
my breath hurt inside my chest
each and every time you kissed me.
What I knew then is what I know now.
I won't say but this one thing.

Now That

you have walked all this way
just to find the ancient pathway

which leads away from,
or was it toward?

the place where I scratched away
the dark layer of a rock's surface

and now that you, traveler,
will take the steps, two by two,

don't slip. It's been a journey
hasn't it?

to have walked all this way
through the city, into the country

on a little-used trail,
climbing over basalt cliffs,

through and beyond the far side
of a shallow wash, down into a valley

overgrown with cholla and saguaro.
Now that you can finally rest,

the bones of both feet hurt,
your mouth is dry.

And now you know what has become
of a mark etched on the wall, a canyon echo

rising up to greet you—
hello?hello!

Notes

The poem title "Teach Me How I Should Forget to Think" is taken from Shakespeare's *Romeo and Juliet*.

"Time flies over us, but leaves its shadow behind." –Nathaniel Hawthorne, *The Marble Faun*

"We travel, some of us forever, to seek other states, other lives, other souls." –Anaïs Nin, *The Diary of Anaïs Nin*

"We are afflicted in every way, but we are not crushed...."
–2 Corinthians 4:8

"Wherever you go, you meet part of your story."–Eudora Welty, *The Art of Fiction*

"Destiny itself is like a wonderful wide tapestry in which every thread is guided by an unspeakably tender hand, placed beside another thread and held and carried by a hundred others."
–Rainer Maria Rilke, *Letters to a Young Poet*

"Our life is composed greatly from dreams, from the unconscious, and they must be brought into connection with action. They must be woven together." – Anaïs Nin*, The Diary of Anaïs Nin*

"Show not what has been done, but what can be. How beautiful the world would be if there were a procedure for moving through labyrinths."–Umberto Eco, *The Name of the Rose*

About the Author

Lois Roma-Deeley's previous full-length poetry collections include: *The Short List of Certainties,* winner of the Jacopone da Todi Book Prize (2017); *High Notes* (2010), a Paterson Poetry Prize Finalist; *northSight* (2006); and *Rules of Hunger* (2004).

Her work is featured in numerous anthologies and journals. She is Poet Laureate of Scottsdale, Arizona (2021–2024). Roma-Deeley is the Associate Editor of the international poetry journal *Presence: A Journal of Catholic Poetry.* She was named U.S. Professor of the Year, Community College, by the Carnegie Foundation for the Advancement of Teaching and CASE, 2012–2013.

She holds an MFA in poetry from Arizona State University and a Ph.D. with a primary emphasis in poetry from The Union Institute and University. She lives in Scottsdale, Arizona, with her family.

loisroma-deeley.com

www.ingramcontent.com/pod-product-compliance
Lightning Source LLC
Chambersburg PA
CBHW070549090426
42735CB00013B/3123